MINI-SIZED
WRITE-YOUR-OWN
COMIC BOOK

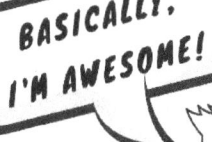
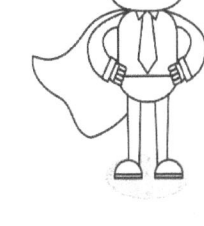
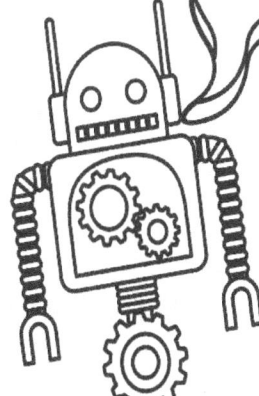
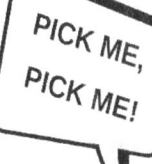
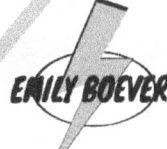

EMILY BOEVER

For More Fun Products,

Go To:

TheClassicalThing.com

All rights reserved. No part of this work may be reproduced, stored in a retrieval system, or transmitted in any form or by any means, electronic, mechanical, photocopying, recording, or otherwise, without prior written permission of the author.

Write-Your-Own Comic Book: Mini Sized
October 2018
Copyright © 2018 Emily Boever
ISBN: 9781726805896

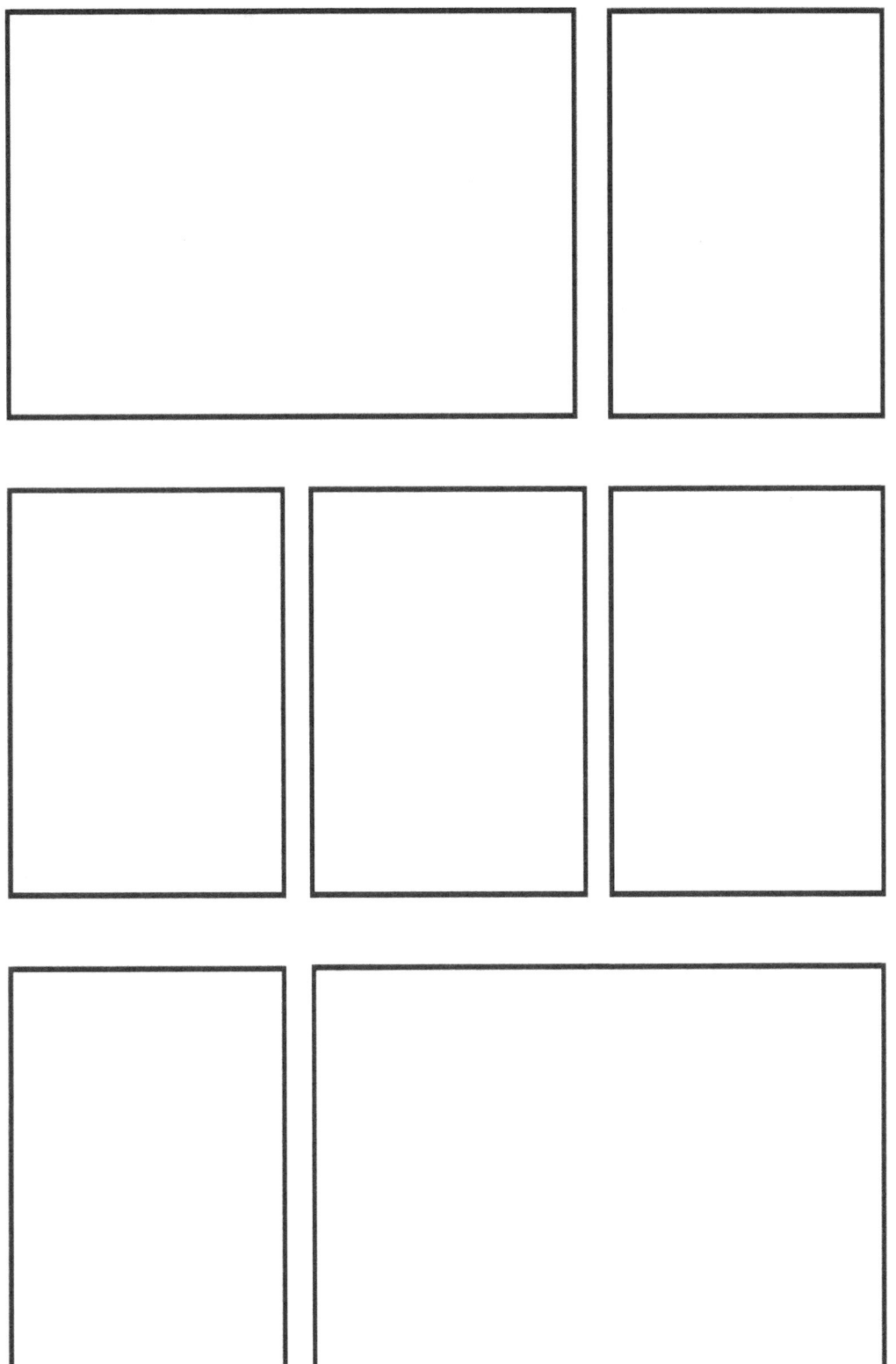

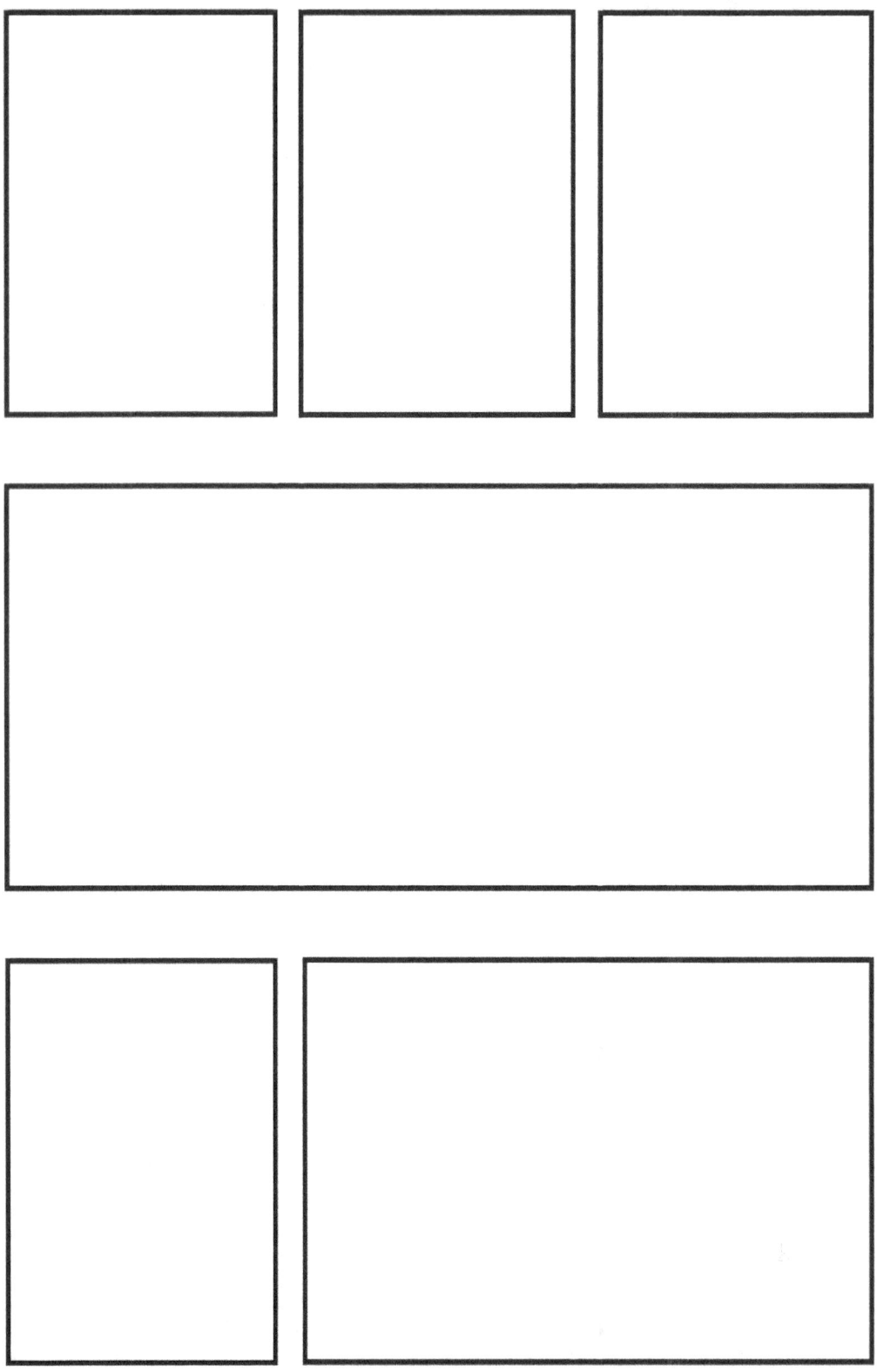

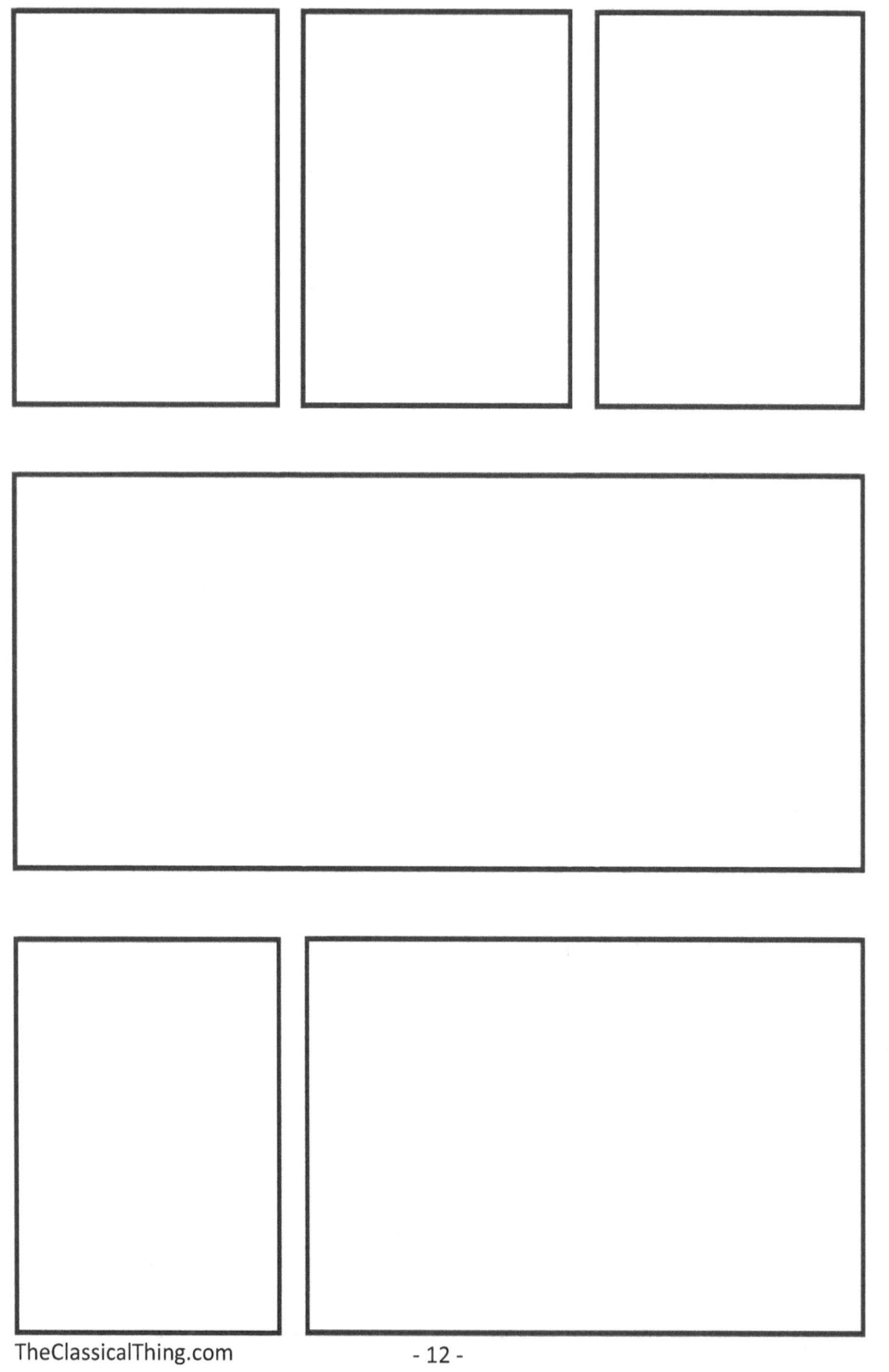

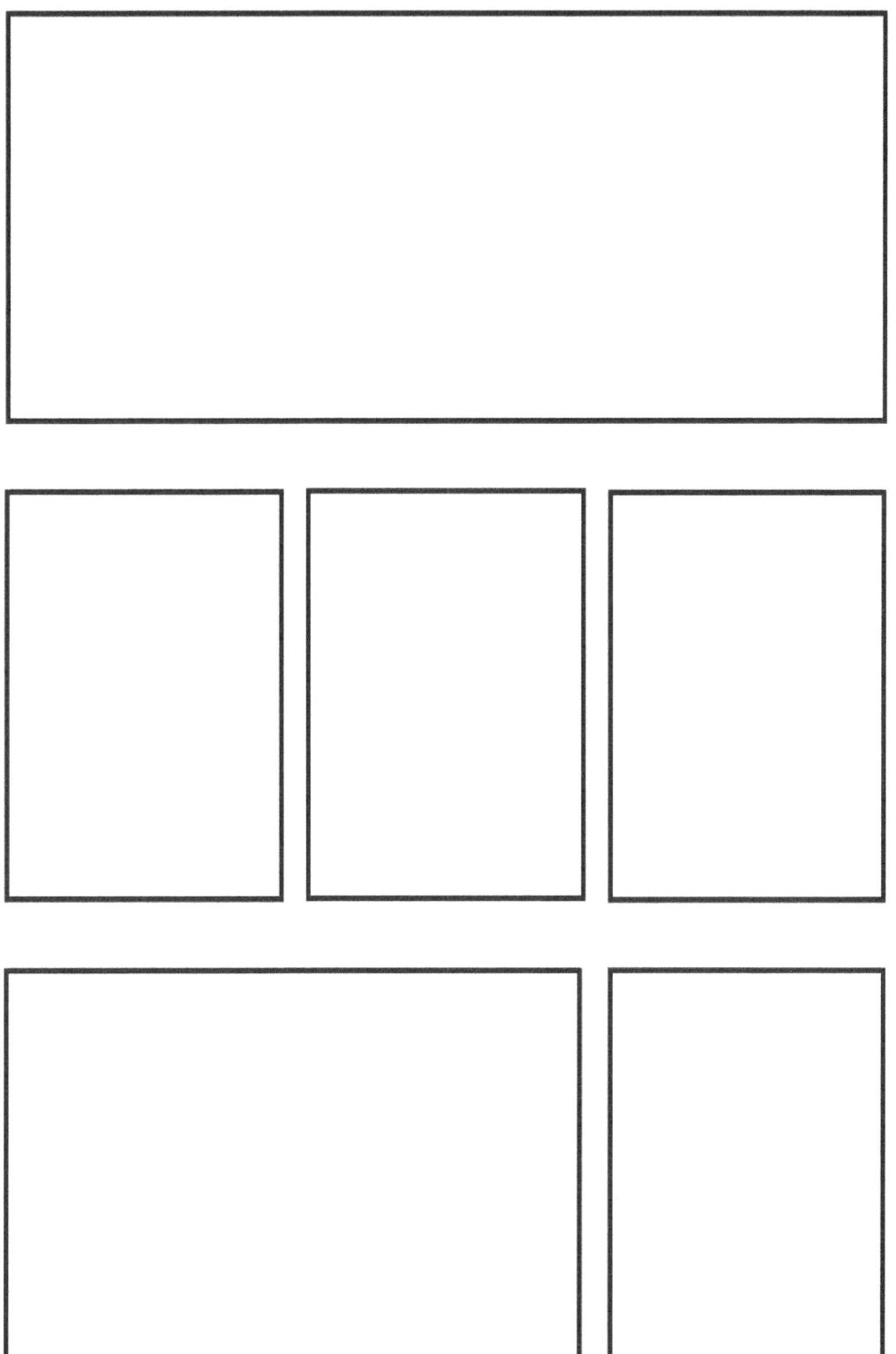

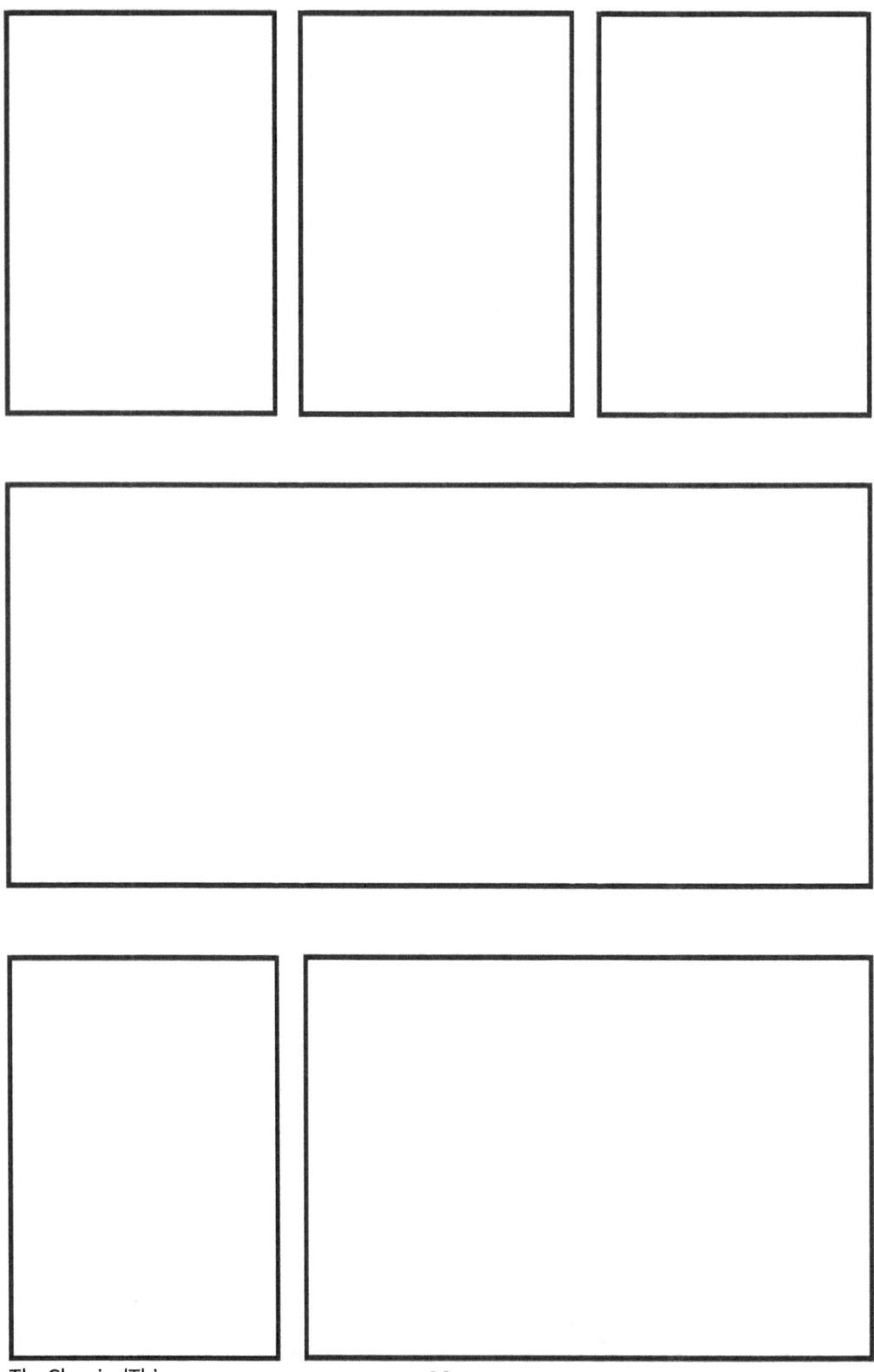

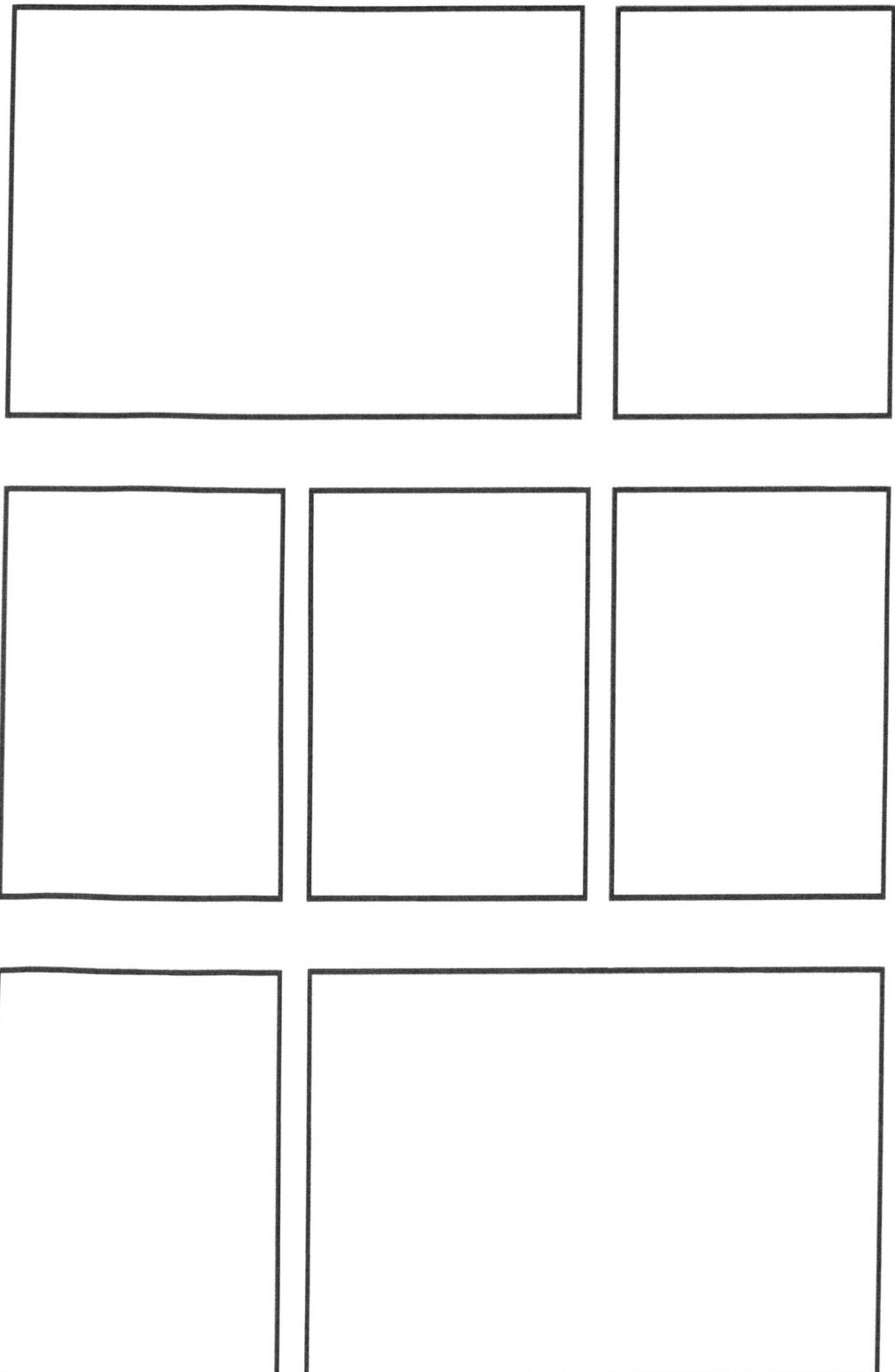

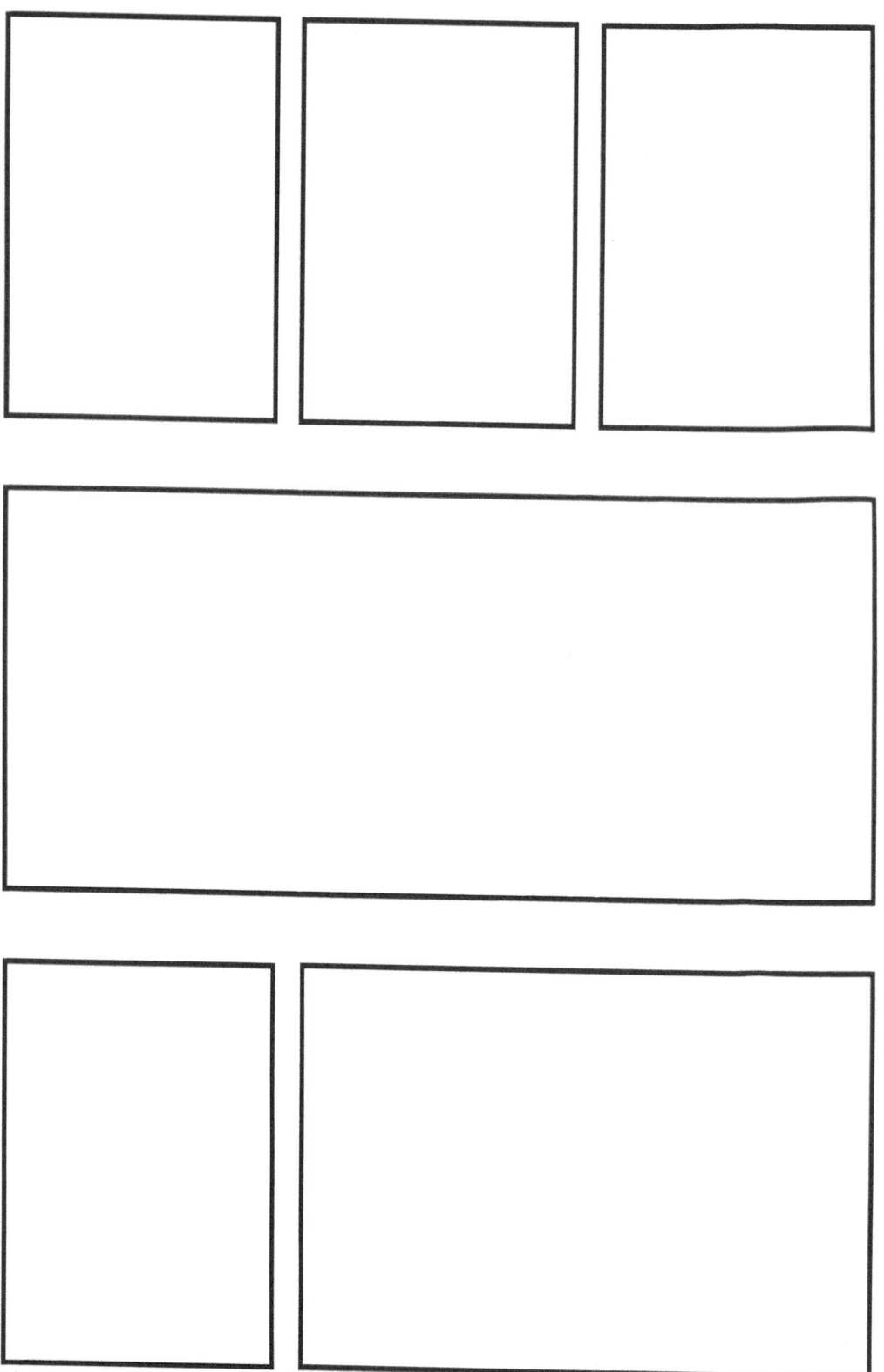

TheClassicalThing.com

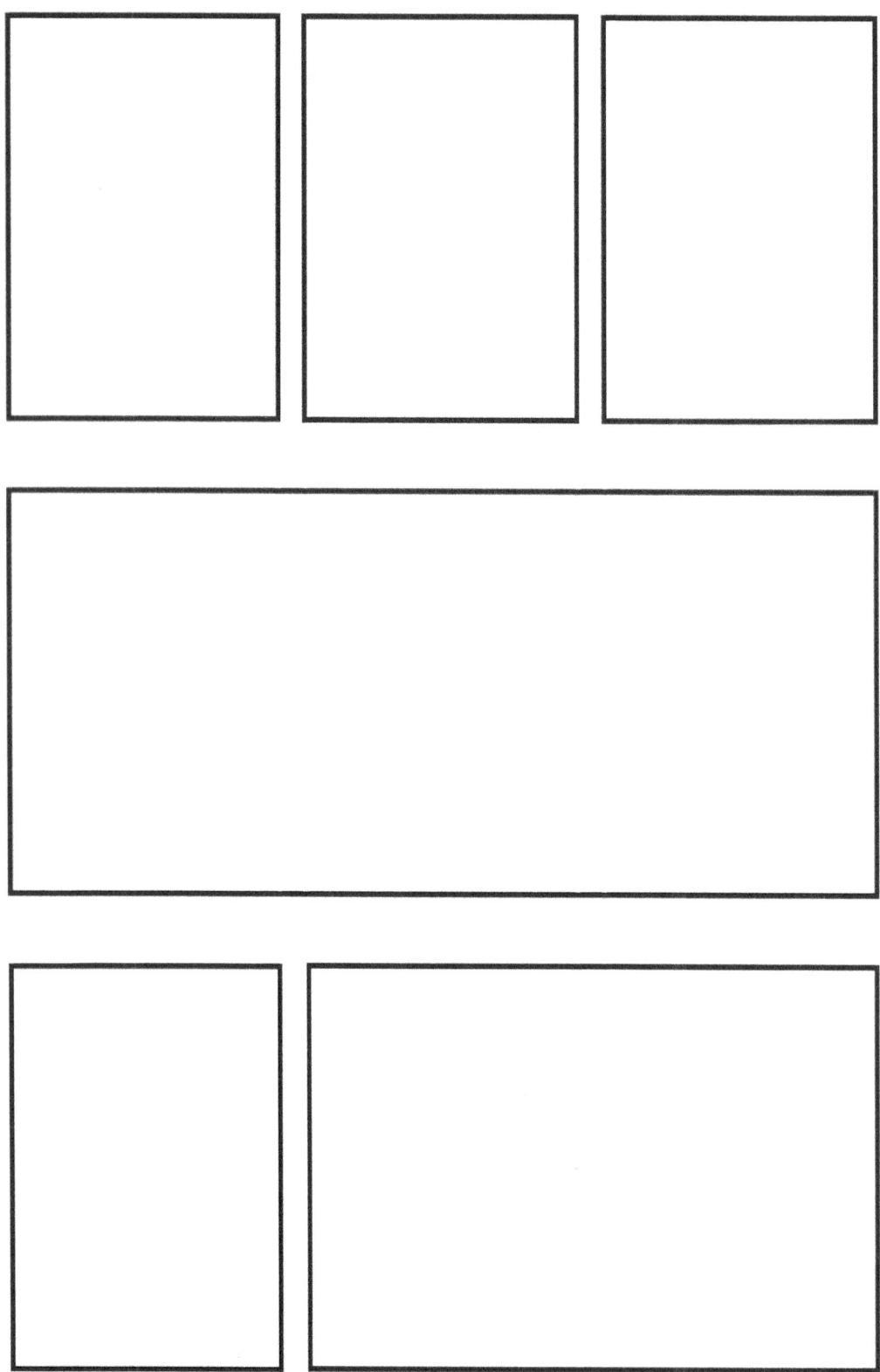

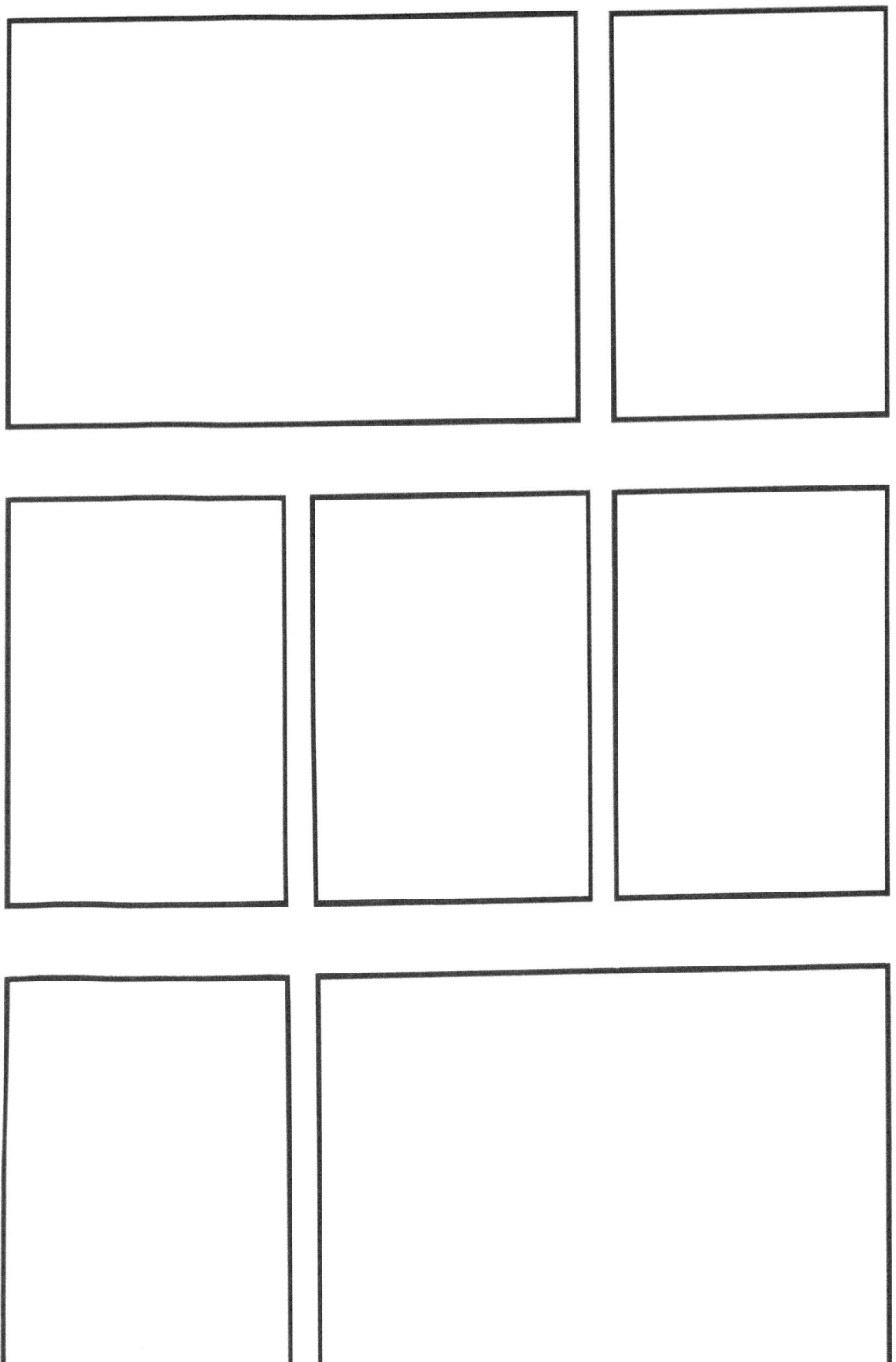

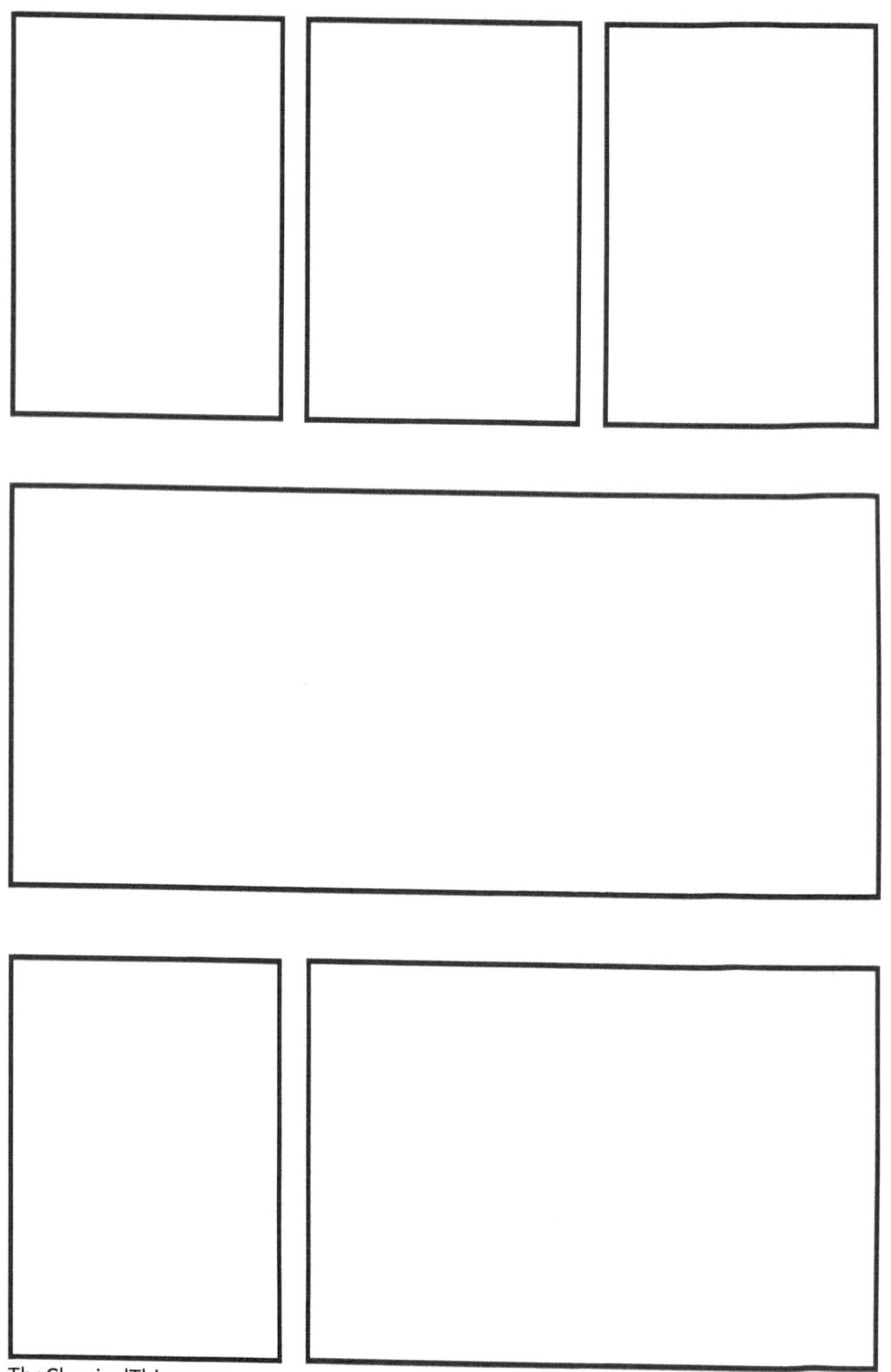

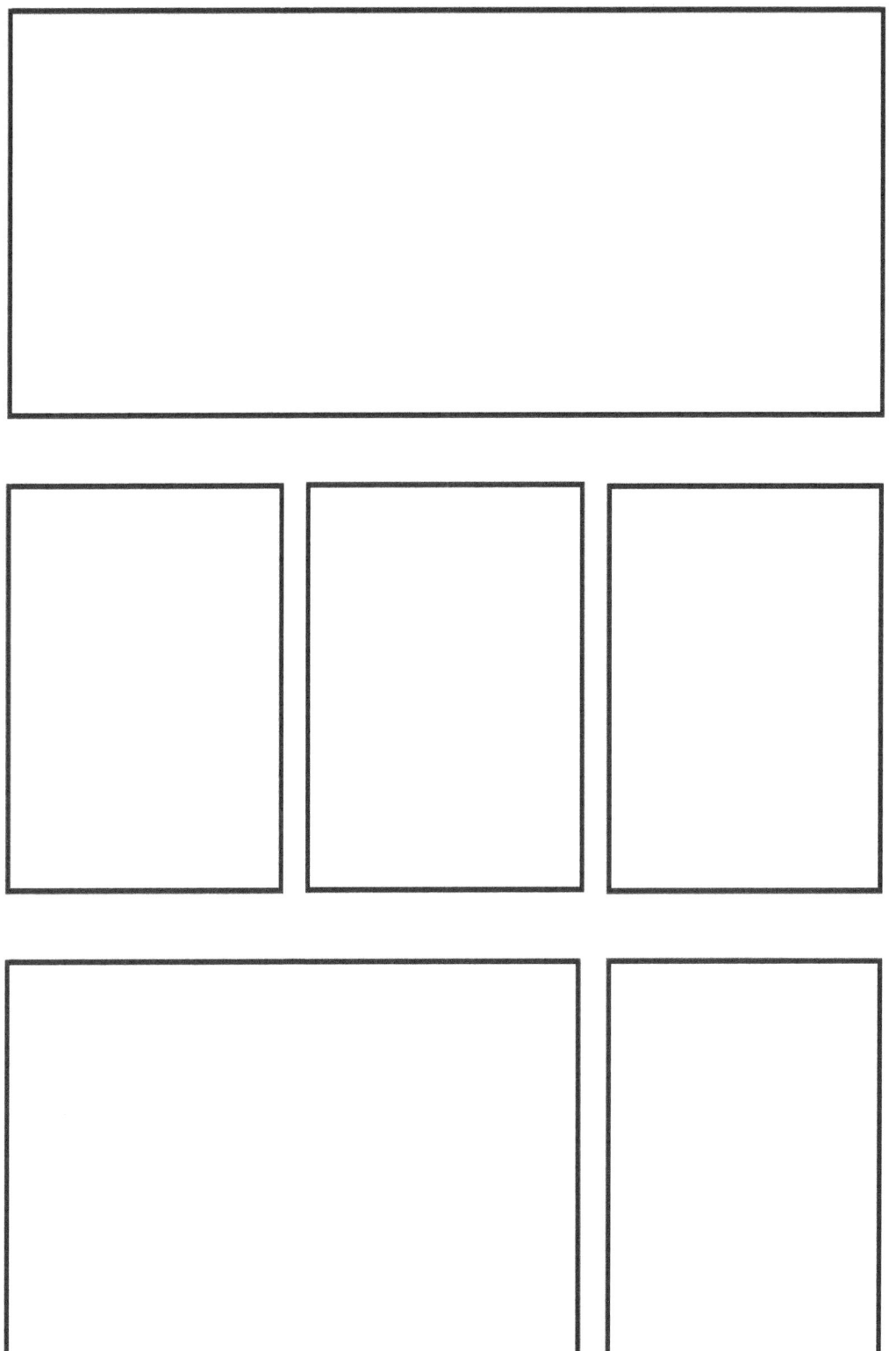

TheClassicalThing.com - 38 -

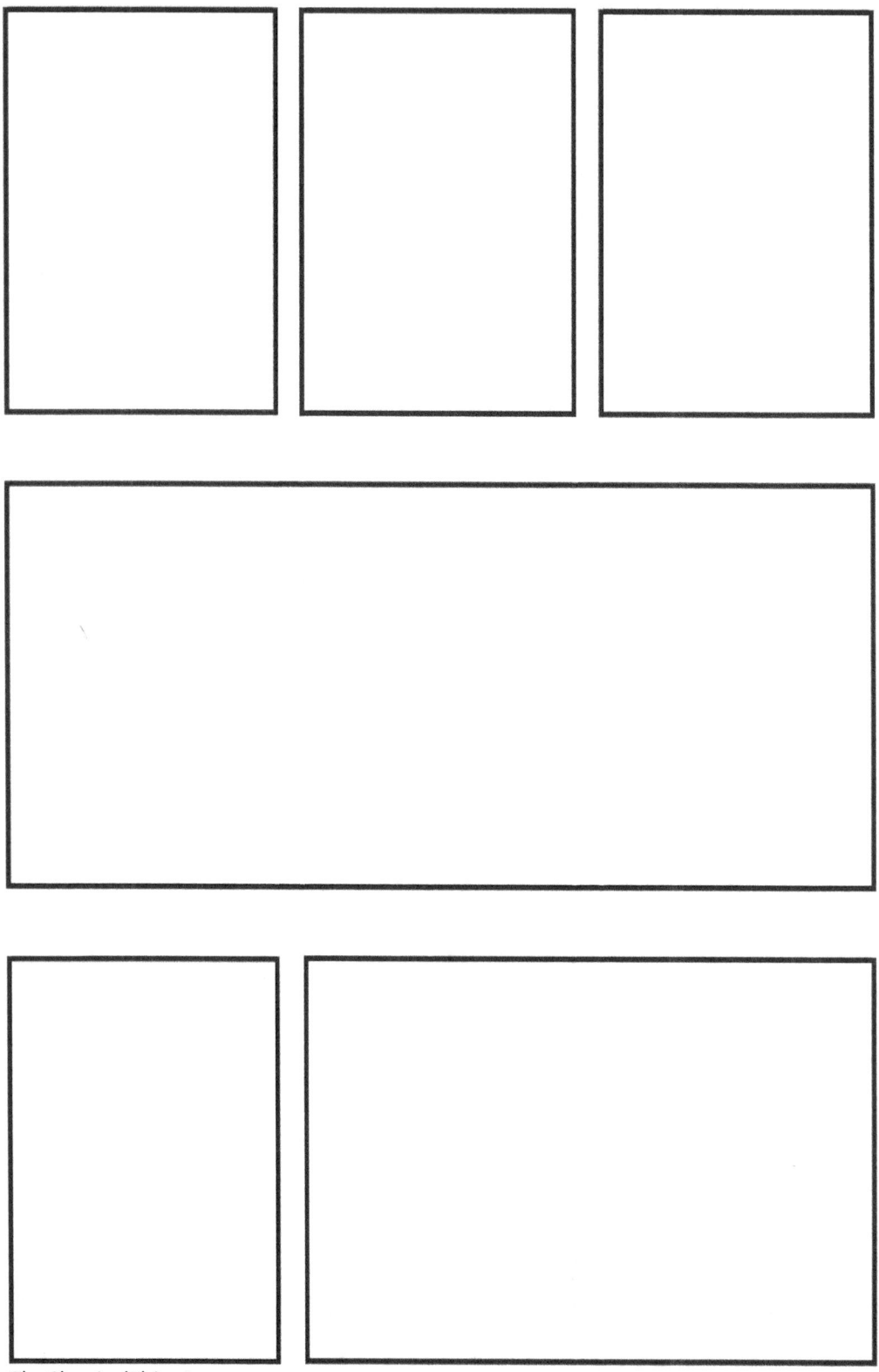

TheClassicalThing.com

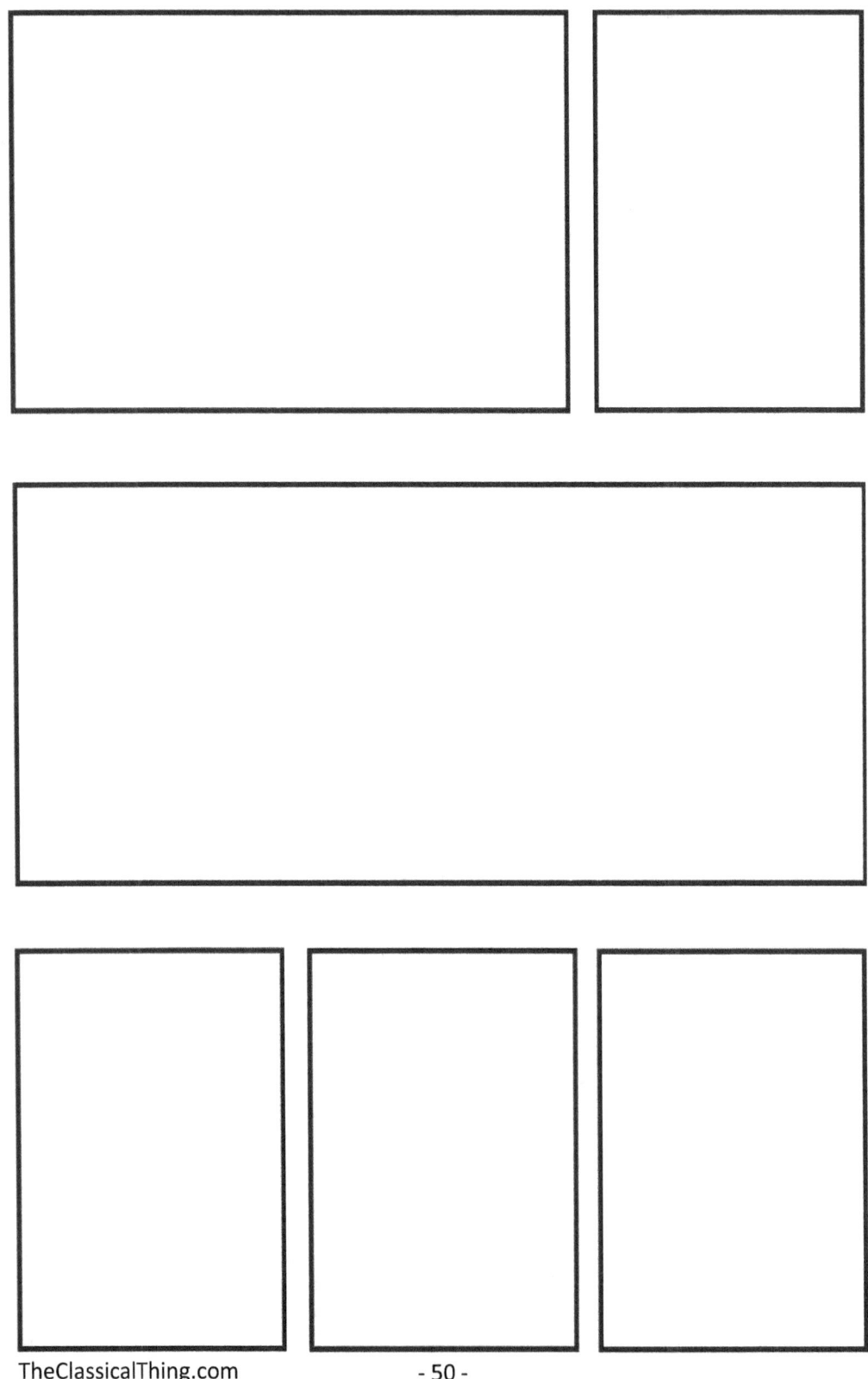

TheClassicalThing.com

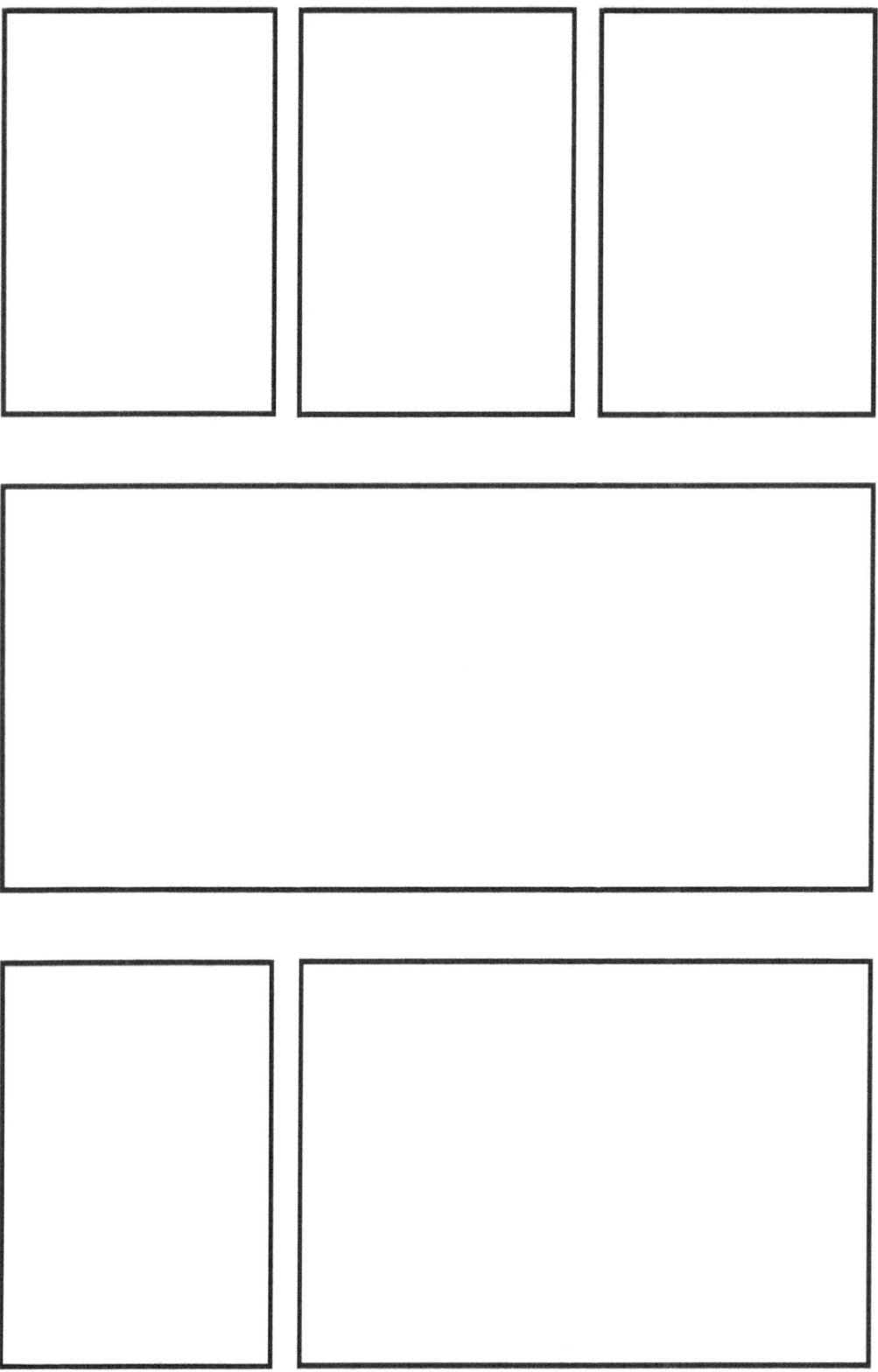

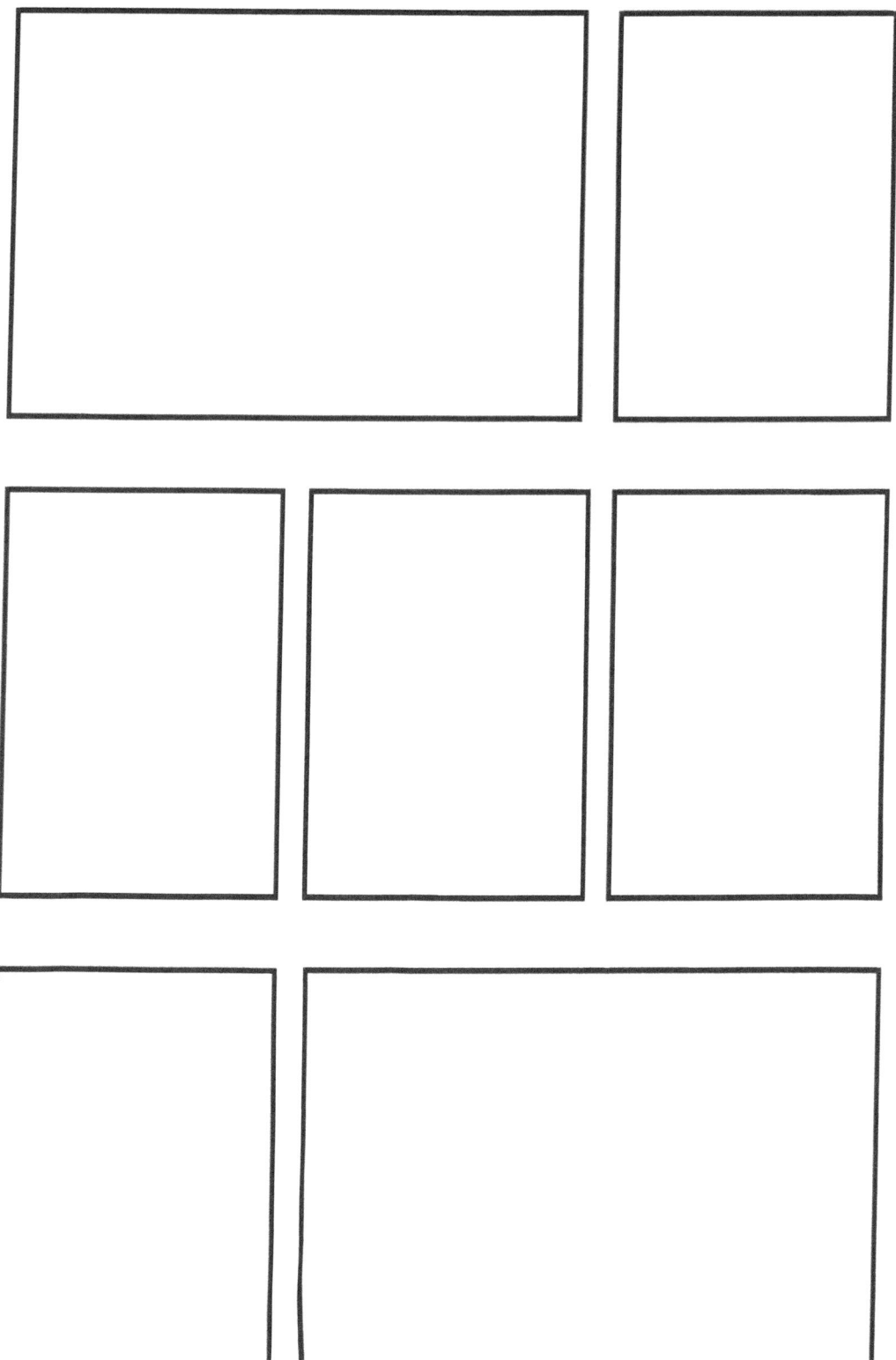

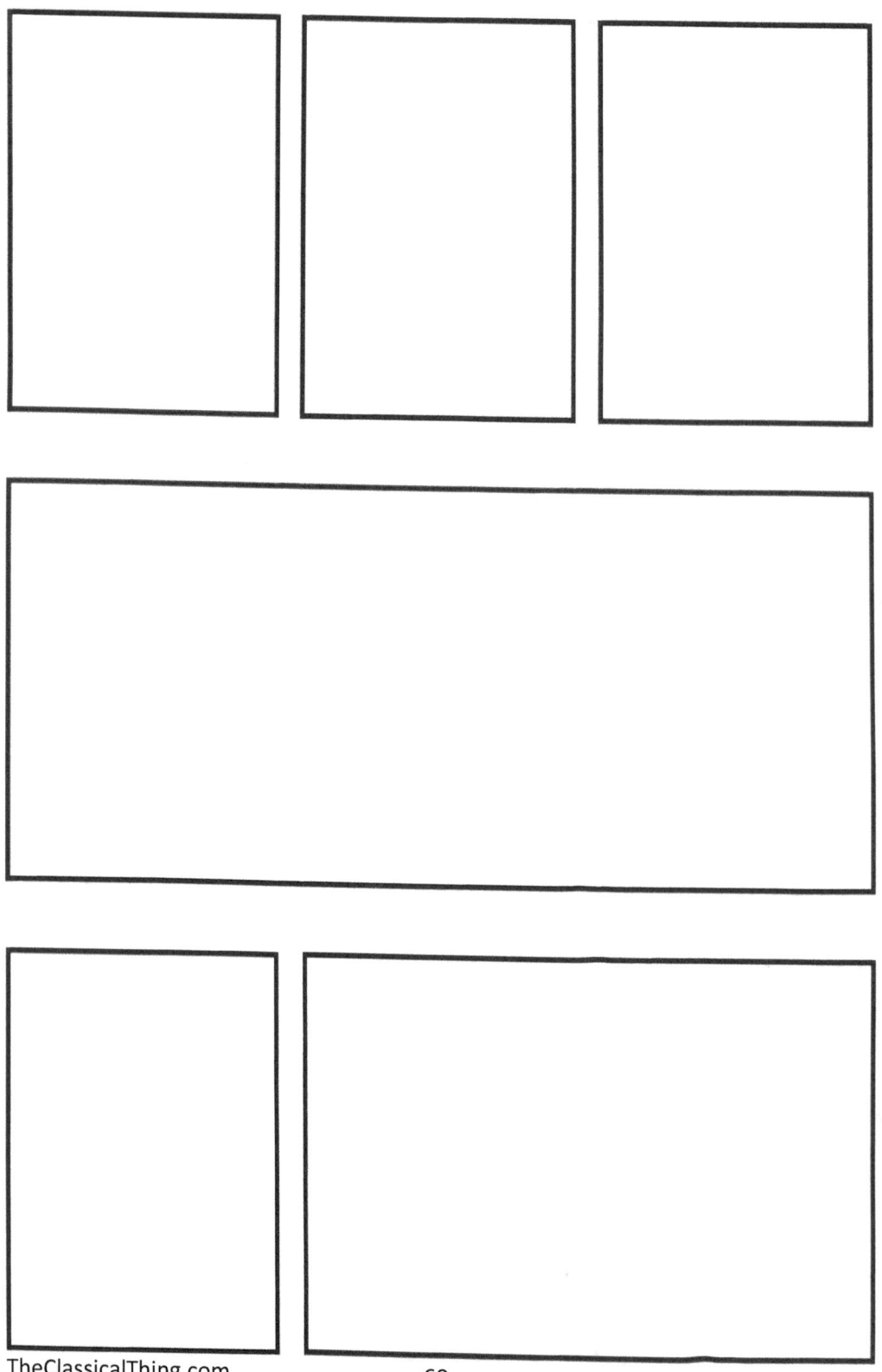

TheClassicalThing.com

TheClassicalThing.com

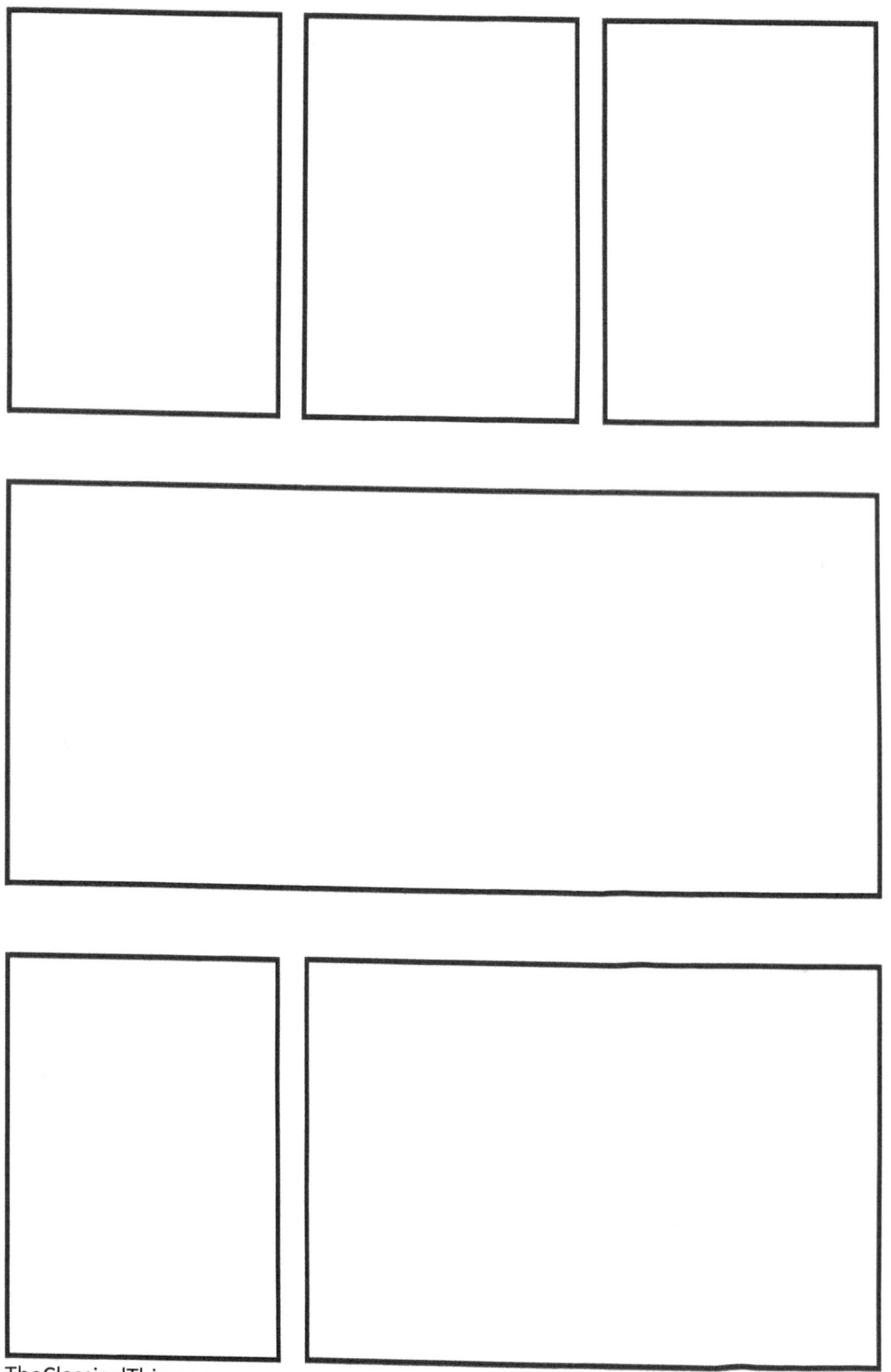

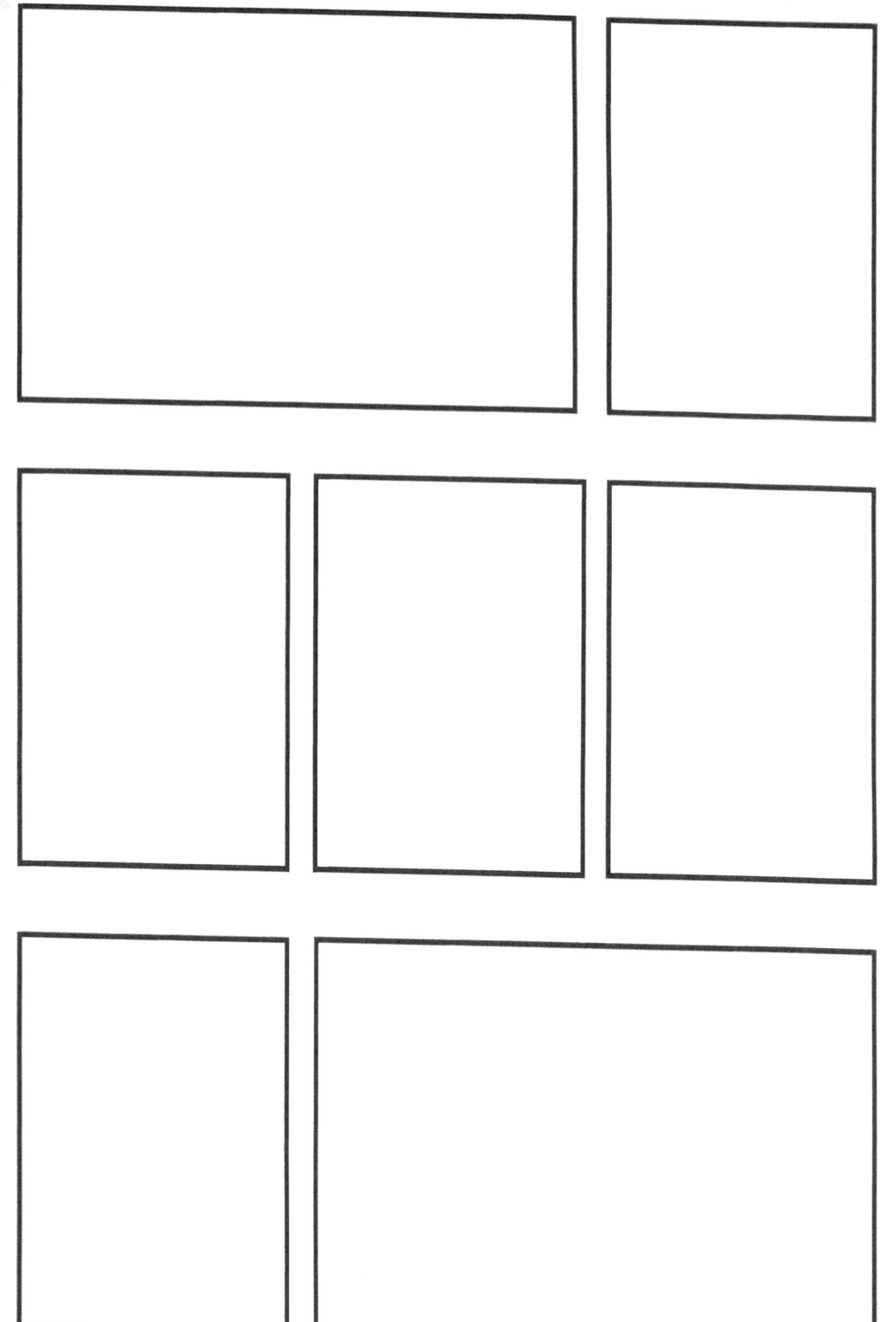

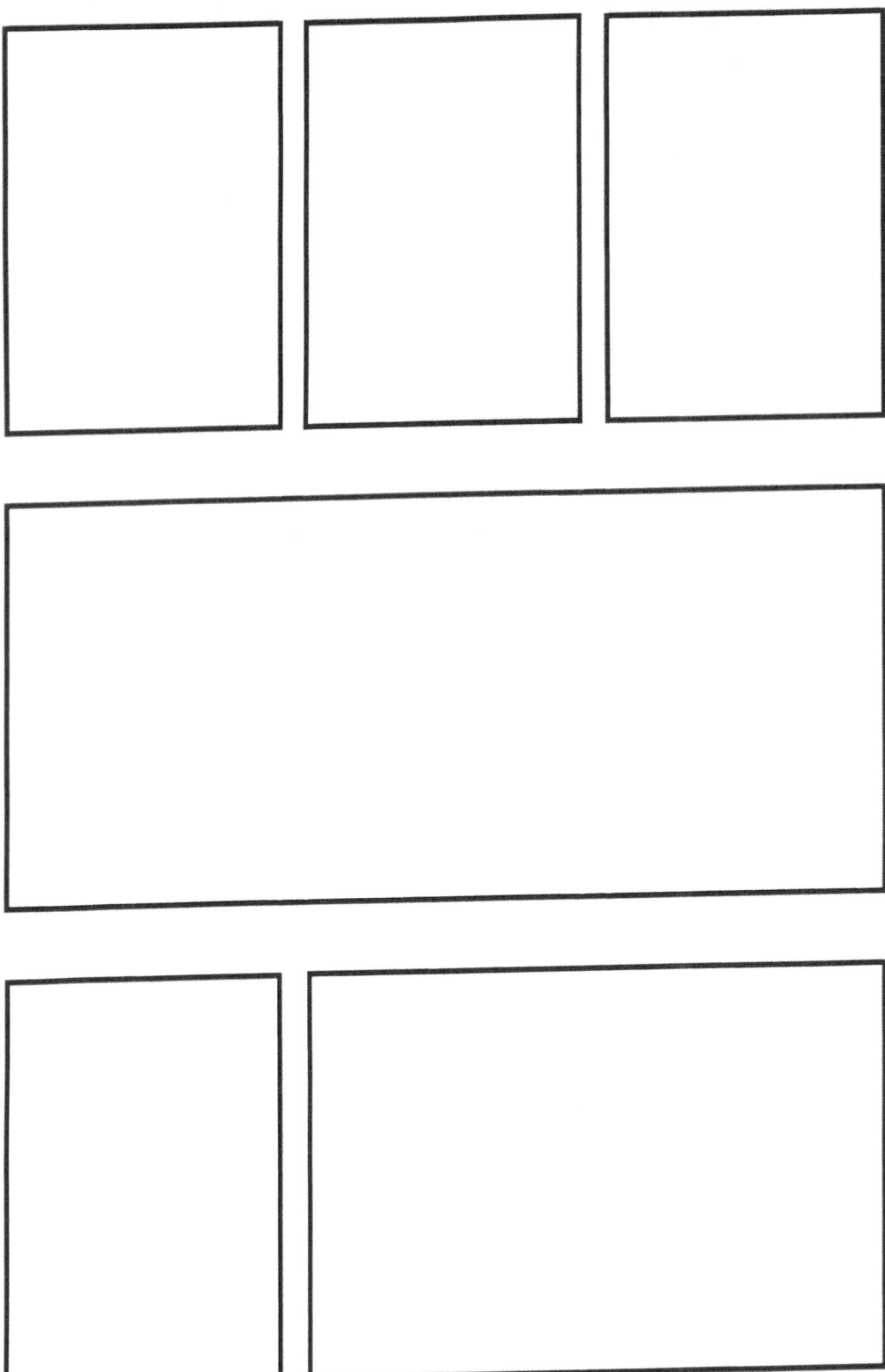

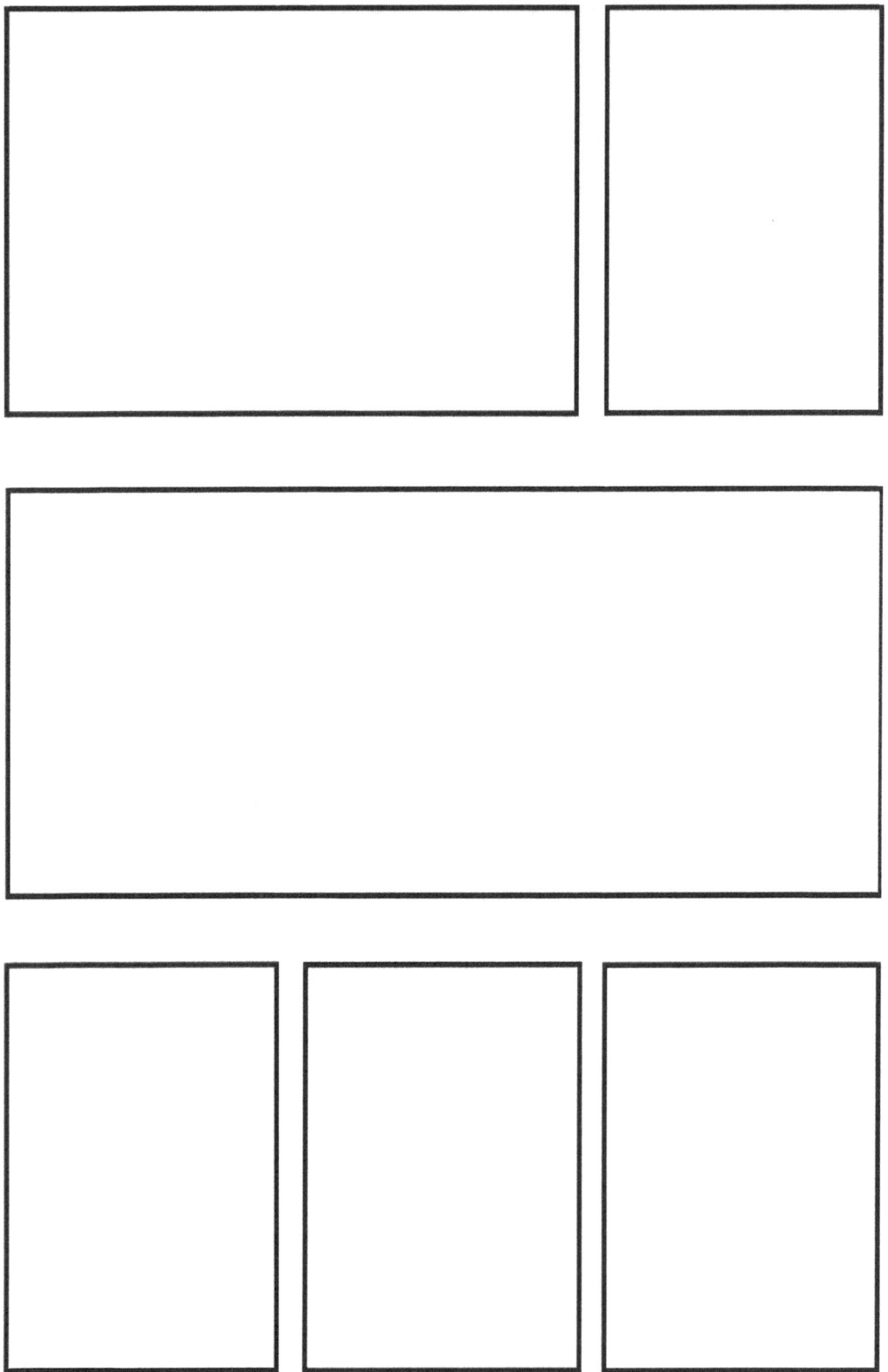

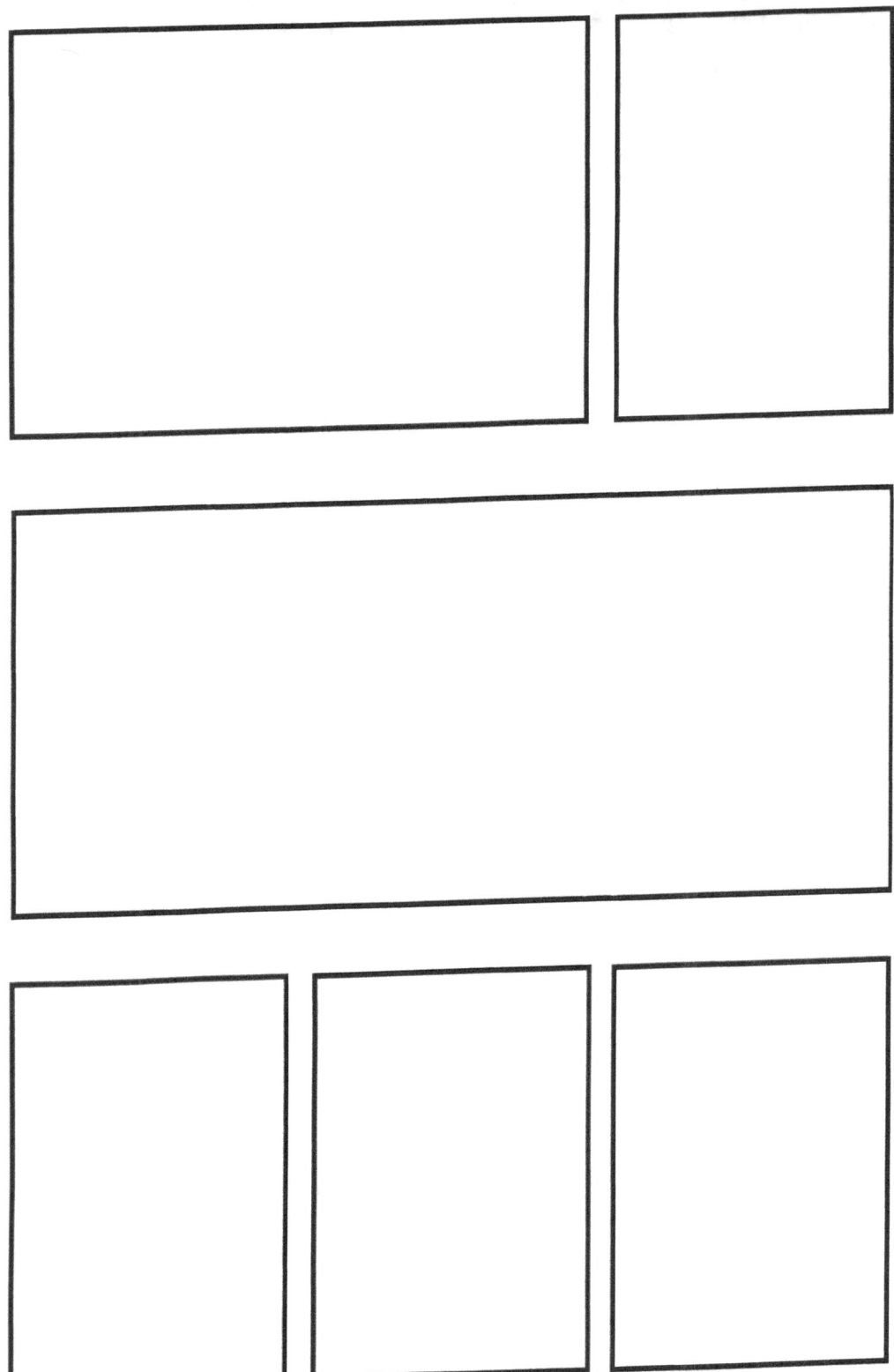

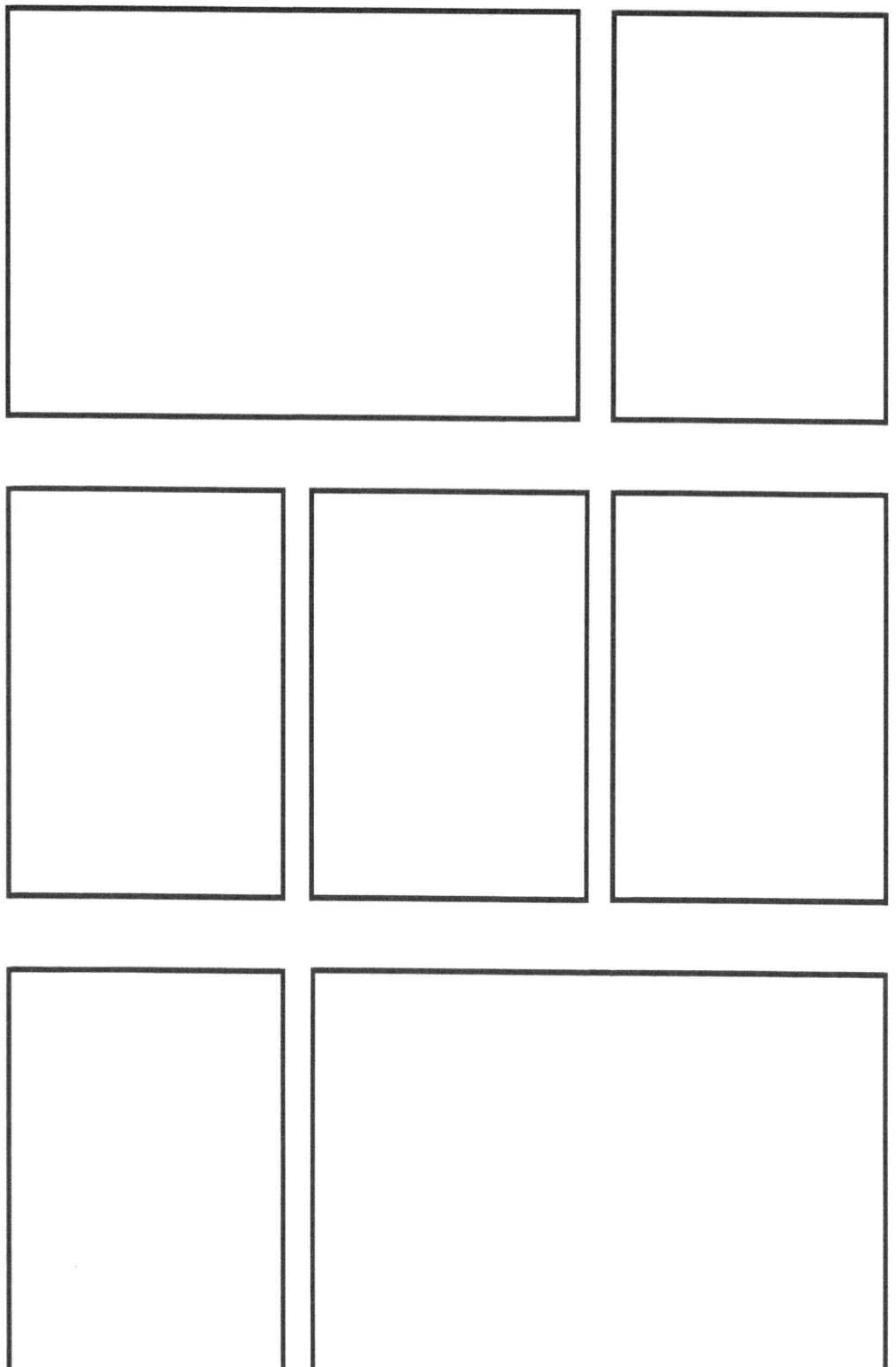

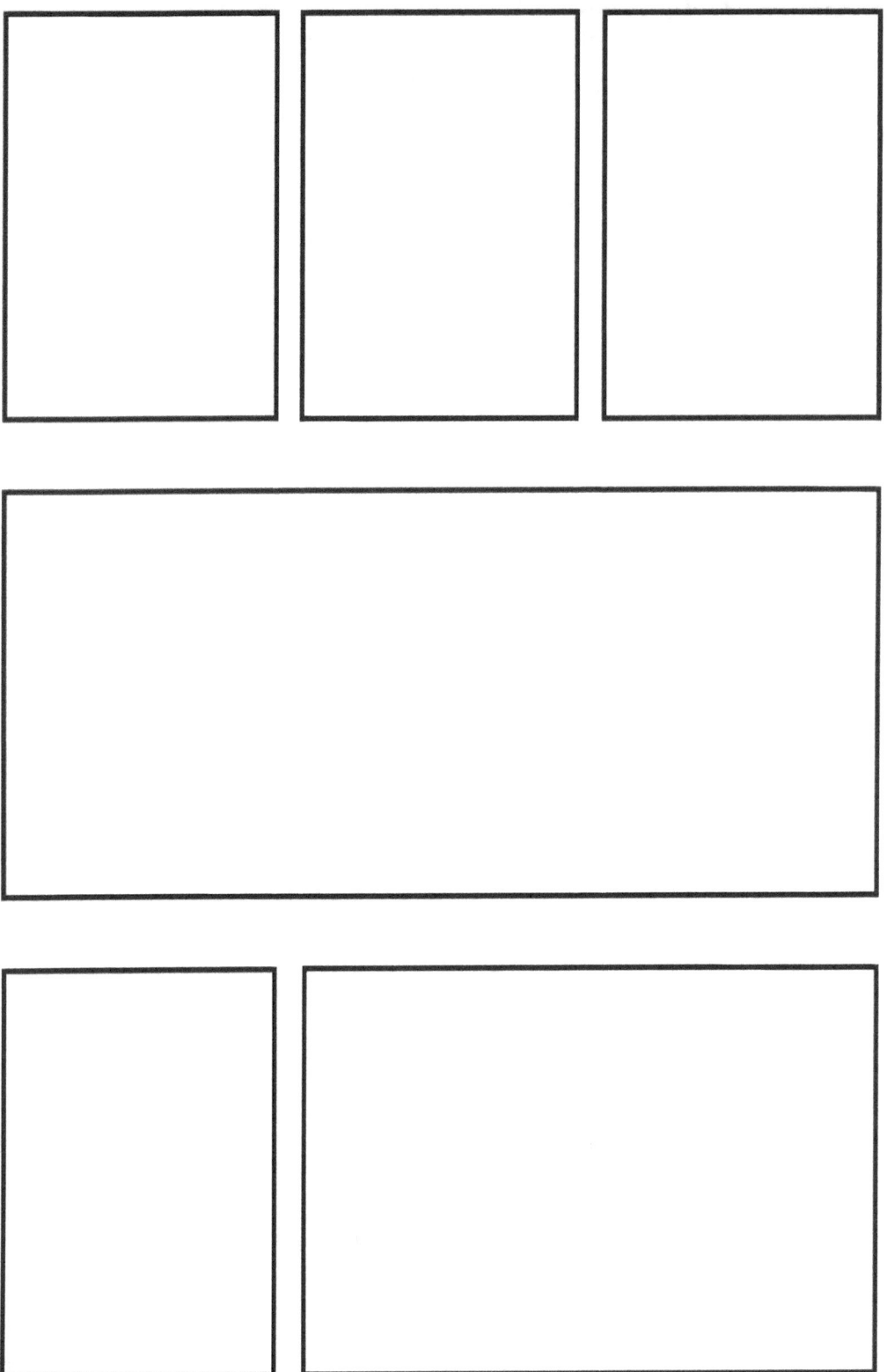

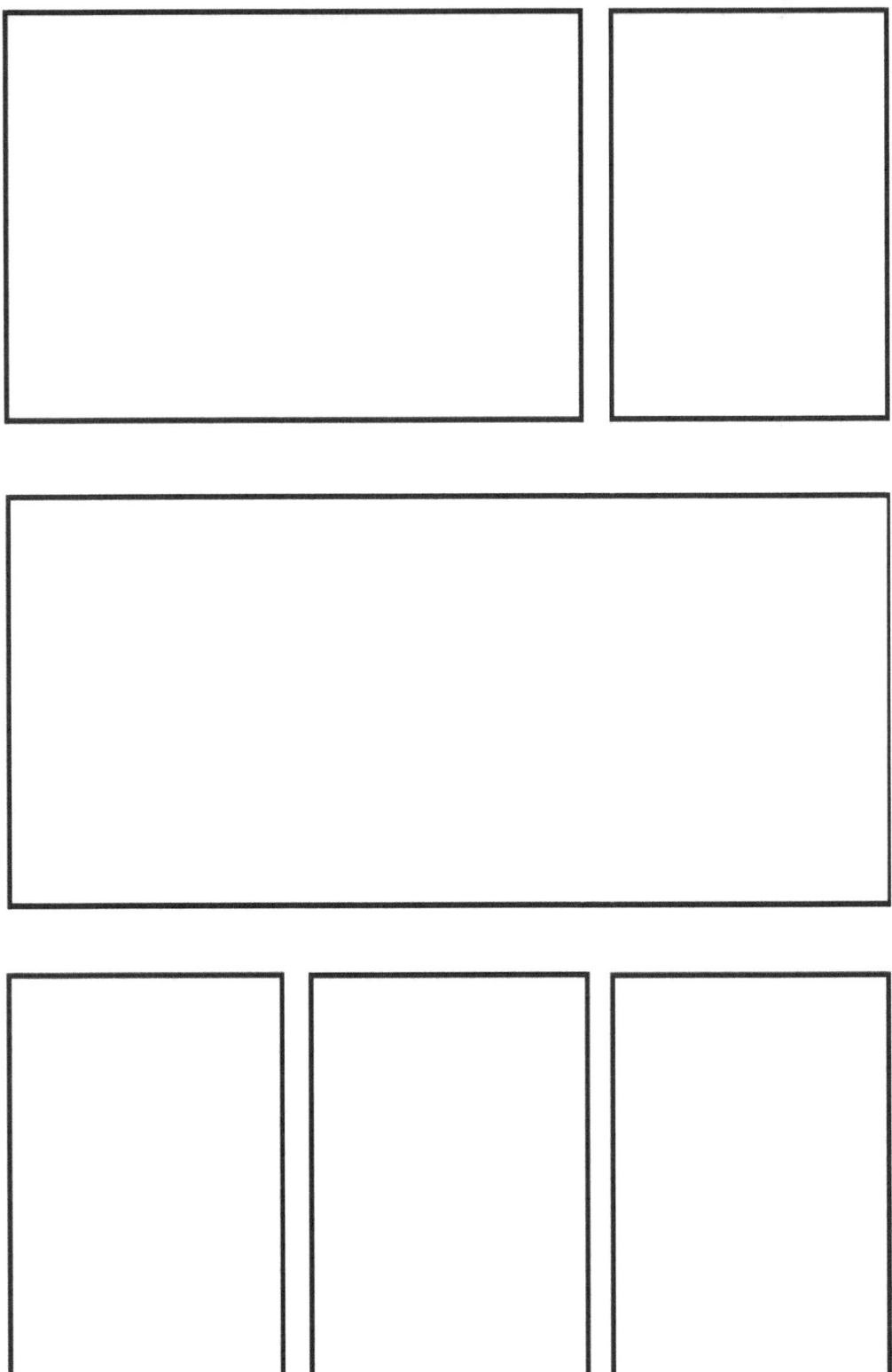

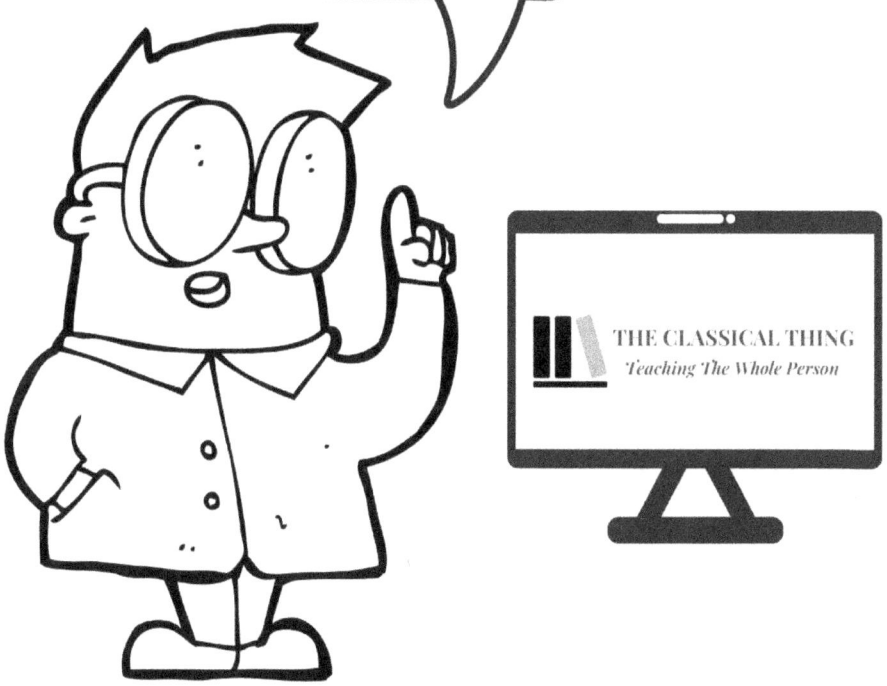

www.ingramcontent.com/pod-product-compliance
Lightning Source LLC
Chambersburg PA
CBHW071411220526
45469CB00004B/1250